CHRISTMAS AT OUR HOUSE

CHRISTMAS AT OUR HOUSE

A Family Memory Book

Illustrated by Mona Conner

A Promised Land Production

1817

HARPER & ROW, PUBLISHERS, New York
Cambridge, Philadelphia, San Francisco, London
Mexico City, São Paulo, Singapore, Sydney

For Grandma "Peg" Conner.
If only you could see what you started.

M.D.C.

CHRISTMAS AT OUR HOUSE.

FIRST EDITION

Type Design: John Lynch

86 87 88 89 90 10 9 8 7 6 5 4 3 2 1

Christmas at Our House was given to _____

by _____ on _____

This book was started in time for Christmas 19____

by the _____ family

who live at _____

Our family members are _____

_____

_____

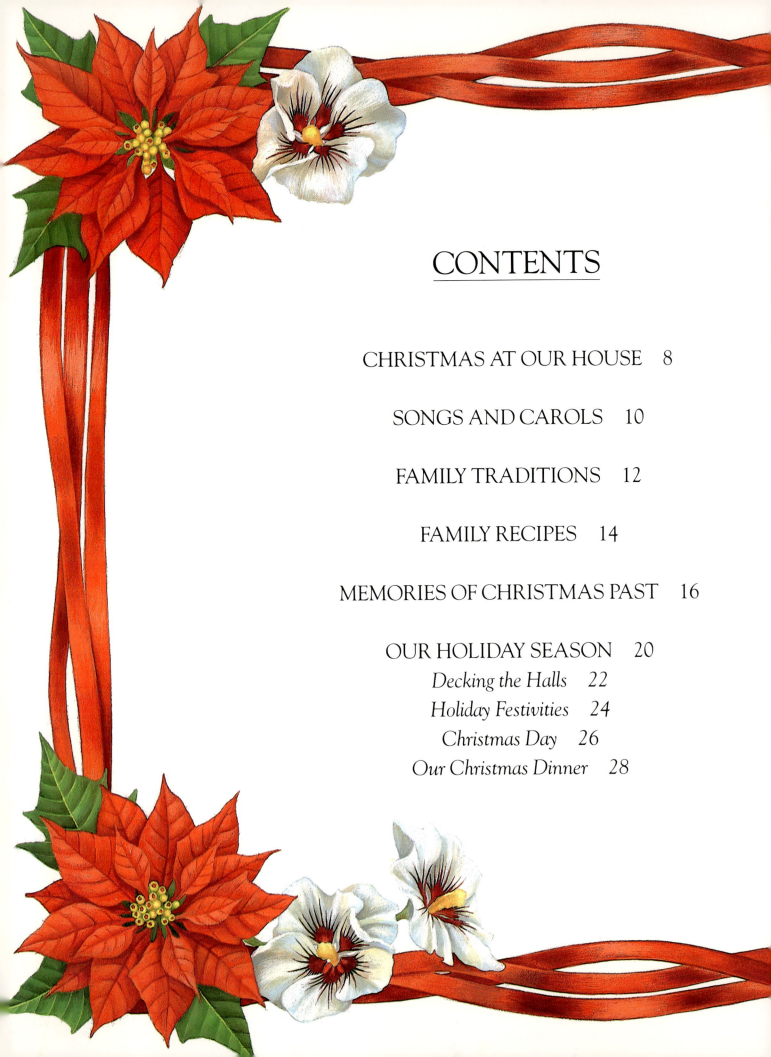

CONTENTS

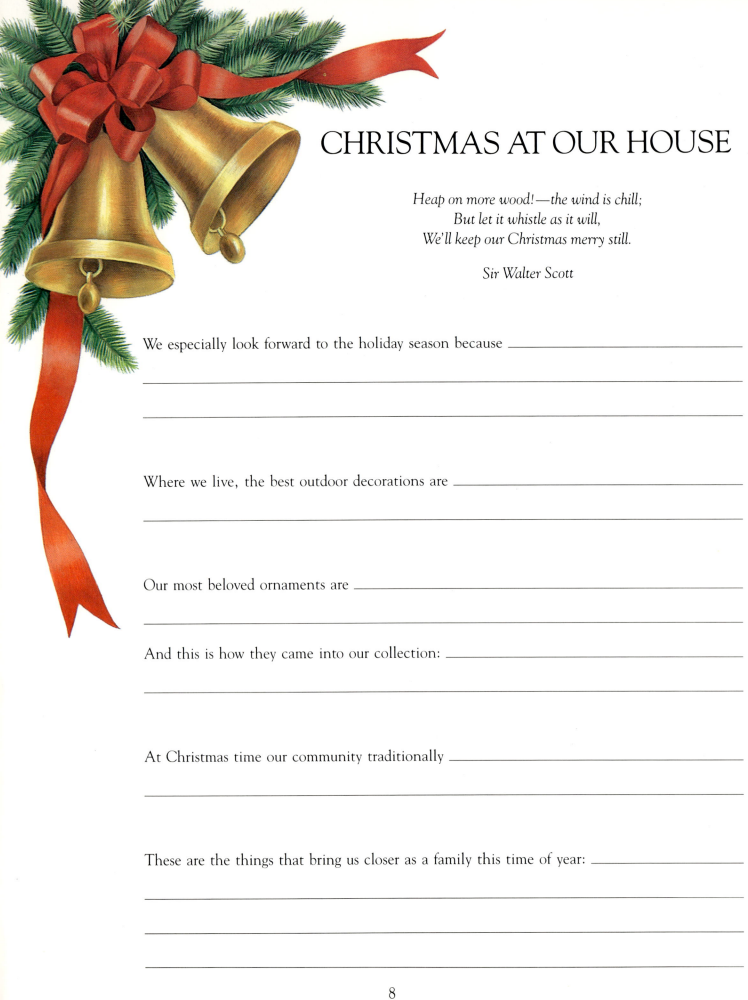

CHRISTMAS AT OUR HOUSE

Heap on more wood!—the wind is chill;
But let it whistle as it will,
We'll keep our Christmas merry still.

Sir Walter Scott

We especially look forward to the holiday season because _____

_____

_____

Where we live, the best outdoor decorations are _____

_____

Our most beloved ornaments are _____

_____

And this is how they came into our collection: _____

_____

At Christmas time our community traditionally _____

_____

These are the things that bring us closer as a family this time of year: _____

_____

_____

_____

These are the things that bring us closer to others:

_____

_____

_____

_____

Christmas means many things to many people. This is what it means to each of us:

_____   " _____
name

                                                _____

                                                _____ "

_____   " _____
name

                                                _____

                                                _____ "

_____   " _____
name

                                                _____

                                                _____ "

_____   " _____
name

                                                _____

                                                _____ "

_____   " _____
name

                                                _____

                                                _____ "

_____   " _____
name

                                                _____

                                                _____ "

9

SONGS AND CAROLS

Sing aloud in praise of Christmas,
Bells and birds and happy children. . . .

George Wither

Our family's favorite songs and carols are _____

_____

_____

_____

_____

The music we most associate with the holidays is _____

_____

_____

_____ has the best voice in our family,

but _____ sings with the most gusto.

The records you'd be likely to hear at our house during the Christmas season are _____

_____

_____

CHRISTMAS IS COMING

Traditional

Christmas is coming! The goose is getting fat;
Please to put a penny in an old man's hat.
If you haven't got a penny, a half-penny will do.
If you haven't got a half-penny, then God bless you.

GOOD KING WENCESLAS

Sixteenth-century Carol

Good King Wenceslas looked out
On the feast of Stephen,
When the snow lay round about,
Deep and crisp and even.
Brightly shone the moon that night,
Though the frost was cruel,
When a poor man came in sight,
Gathering winter fuel.

HERE WE COME A-CAROLING

English Wassail Song

Here we come a-caroling
Among the leaves so green;
Here we come a wand'ring
So fair to be seen.
Love and joy come to you
And to you glad Christmas too,
And God bless you and send you
a Happy New Year,
And God send you a Happy New Year.

JOLLY OLD SAINT NICHOLAS

Traditional

Jolly old Saint Nicholas,
Lean your ear this way!
Don't you tell a single soul
What I'm going to say;
Christmas Eve is coming soon;
Now, you dear old man,
Whisper what you'll bring to me;
Tell me if you can.

FAMILY TRADITIONS

Then, high-ho, the holly!
This life is most jolly!

William Shakespeare

For our family, the holiday season really begins when we _____

_____

We mark the weeks before Christmas by _____

_____

_____

The season wouldn't be the same if we didn't _____

_____

_____

We always keep in touch with friends and family by _____

_____

_____

Christmas Eve is the time for _____

_____

_____

And on Christmas day we always _____

_____

_____

The traditions that bring us closer together are _____

_____

_____

These people make the season special in the following ways:

_____ because _____

_____ because _____

_____ because _____

_____ because _____

If you came to our house at Christmas time, you'd be likely

to see _____ ,

hear _____ ,

and smell _____

During the holidays, our family is famous for _____

_____

Other special ways we celebrate the season:

_____

_____

_____

_____

_____

_____

_____

FAMILY RECIPES

Lo! now is come our joyfull'st feast!
Let every man be jolly. . . .

George Wither

Our favorite holiday recipe is _____,

which we learned from _____

Our traditional Christmas treats are _____

_____

_____

_____ 's recipe for _____ :

_____ _____ _____

_____ _____ _____

_____ _____

_____ _____

_____ _____

_____ _____

_____ 's recipe for _____ :

_____ _____ _____

_____ _____ _____

_____ _____

_____ _____

_____ _____

_____ _____

14

_____'s recipe for _____:

_____ _____ _____

_____ _____ _____

_____ _____

_____ _____

_____ _____

_____

_____'s recipe for _____:

_____ _____ _____

_____ _____ _____

_____ _____

_____ _____

_____ _____

_____

MEMORIES OF CHRISTMAS PAST

I heard the bells on Christmas Day
Their old familiar carols play
And wild and sweet
The word repeat
Of peace on earth, good-will to men!

Henry Wadsworth Longfellow

Stories about the holidays we've heard from our

grandparents and other family members: ____

_____

_____

_____

_____

_____

_____

_____

_____

_____

_____

_____

_____

_____

_____

_____

_____

_____

_____

_____

_____

_____

_____

_____

_____

_____

_____

_____

_____

Some special childhood memories of Christmas: _____
_____
_____
_____

We best remember the Christmas of _____ because _____
_____
_____

Over the years the people we've shared our festivities with were _____
_____
_____
_____

Our best Christmas Eve was spent _____
_____
_____

We most loved to celebrate Christmas at _____
_____
_____

The family Christmas story we most like to tell is _____

_____

_____

_____

Our most memorable holiday meal was _____

_____

The most fabulous Christmas dessert was _____

_____

Our prettiest tree was decorated with _____

_____

Thoughts and feelings we associate with Christmas at our house: _____

_____

_____

_____

_____

_____

OUR HOLIDAY SEASON

YEAR

*I will honor Christmas in my heart
and try to keep it all the year.*

Charles Dickens,
A Christmas Carol

The events that made this year special were _____

_____

_____

We opened the holiday season by _____

_____

_____

This year we got our house ready for the holidays by _____

_____

_____

_____

DECKING THE HALLS

The tree we chose this year was a _____ ,

and it was _____ feet tall.

We picked the tree because _____

Helping us decorate were _____

_____

_____

This year we added these new ornaments:

_____

_____

_____

_____

_____

_____

And this is what it looked like:

What made the tree especially beautiful was _____

_____

We celebrated our tree trimming by _____

_____

_____

Other special holiday decorations and arrangements were: _____

_____

_____

_____

HOLIDAY FESTIVITIES

Parties and dinners: _____

_____

_____

_____

_____

Visits and visitors: _____

_____

_____

_____

_____

_____

The best moment came when _____

_____

_____

The prettiest decorations we saw were _____

_____

_____

The best food was _____ served

by _____

Our favorite Christmas card was sent by _____

The best "glad tidings" we received were _____

_____

_____

We really felt the spirit of Christmas when _____

_____

_____

The night before Christmas we _____

_____

_____

CHRISTMAS DAY

Christmas Day fell on a _____ this year, and

the weather was _____

_____ was up first and woke everyone

at _____ o'clock.

Joining us for Christmas were _____

_____

_____

_____

Friends and family who were with us in spirit: _____

_____

The first member of the family to open a present was _____ ,

who received a _____

from _____

Gifts that made this Christmas special were:

_____   _____   _____
          gift   *recipient*   *giver*

_____   _____   _____
          gift   *recipient*   *giver*

_____   _____   _____
          gift   *recipient*   *giver*

_____   _____   _____
          gift   *recipient*   *giver*

The greatest surprise came when _____

_____

This year we spent Christmas day by _____

_____

_____

Our wish for others on this Christmas day: _____

_____

What we will always remember about today is _____

_____

OUR CHRISTMAS DINNER

The meal was prepared by _____

_____

Joining us for dinner were _____

_____

_____

The table was set with _____

_____

The holiday decorations at the table were _____

_____

Everyone agreed that the best dish was _____

_____

What made the dinner special was _____

_____

The perfect ending to a wonderful day was _____

_____

THE
MENU

APPETIZERS: _____

_____

_____

MAIN COURSE: _____

_____

_____

_____

_____

_____

_____

BEVERAGES: _____

_____

_____

DESSERT: _____

_____

_____

OUR HOLIDAY SEASON

Y E A R

At Christmas play and make good cheer,
For Christmas comes but once a year.

Thomas Tusser

The events that made this year special were _____

_____

_____

We opened the holiday season by _____

_____

_____

This year we got our house ready for the holidays by _____

_____

_____

DECKING THE HALLS

The tree we chose this year was a _____,

and it was _____ feet tall.

We picked the tree because _____

_____

Helping us decorate were _____

_____

_____

This year we added these new ornaments: _____

_____

_____

_____

What made the tree especially beautiful was

_____

_____

_____

And this is what it looked like:

We celebrated our tree trimming by _____

_____

_____

_____

_____

_____

Other special holiday decorations and arrange-

ments were: _____

_____

_____

_____

_____

_____

_____

HOLIDAY FESTIVITIES

Parties and dinners: _____

_____

_____

_____

_____

Visits and visitors: _____

_____

_____

                                                _____

                                                _____

                                                _____

                                                _____

                                                _____

                                                _____

                                                _____

The best moment came when _____

_____

_____

The prettiest decorations we saw were _____

_____

_____

The best food was _____ served

by _____

Our favorite Christmas card was sent by _____

The best "glad tidings" we received were _____

_____

_____

We really felt the spirit of Christmas when _____

_____

_____

The night before Christmas we _____

_____

_____

CHRISTMAS DAY

Christmas Day fell on a _____ this year, and

the weather was _____

_____ was up first and woke everyone

at _____ o'clock.

Joining us for Christmas were _____

_____

_____

_____

_____

Friends and family who were with us in spirit: _____

_____

_____

_____

The first member of the family to open a present was _____ ,

who received a _____

from _____

Gifts that made this Christmas special were:

_____	_____	_____
gift	*recipient*	*giver*
_____	_____	_____
gift	*recipient*	*giver*
_____	_____	_____
gift	*recipient*	*giver*
_____	_____	_____
gift	*recipient*	*giver*

The greatest surprise came when _____

_____

This year we spent Christmas day by _____

_____

_____

_____

Our wish for others on this Christmas day: _____

_____

_____

What we will always remember about today is _____

_____

_____

OUR CHRISTMAS DINNER

The meal was prepared by _____

_____

Joining us for dinner were _____

_____

_____

The table was set with _____

_____

The holiday decorations at the table were _____

_____

Everyone agreed that the best dish was _____

_____

What made the dinner special was _____

_____

The perfect ending to a wonderful day was _____

_____

THE
MENU

Appetizers: _____

_____

_____

Main Course: _____

_____

_____

_____

_____

_____

Beverages: _____

_____

_____

Dessert: _____

_____

_____

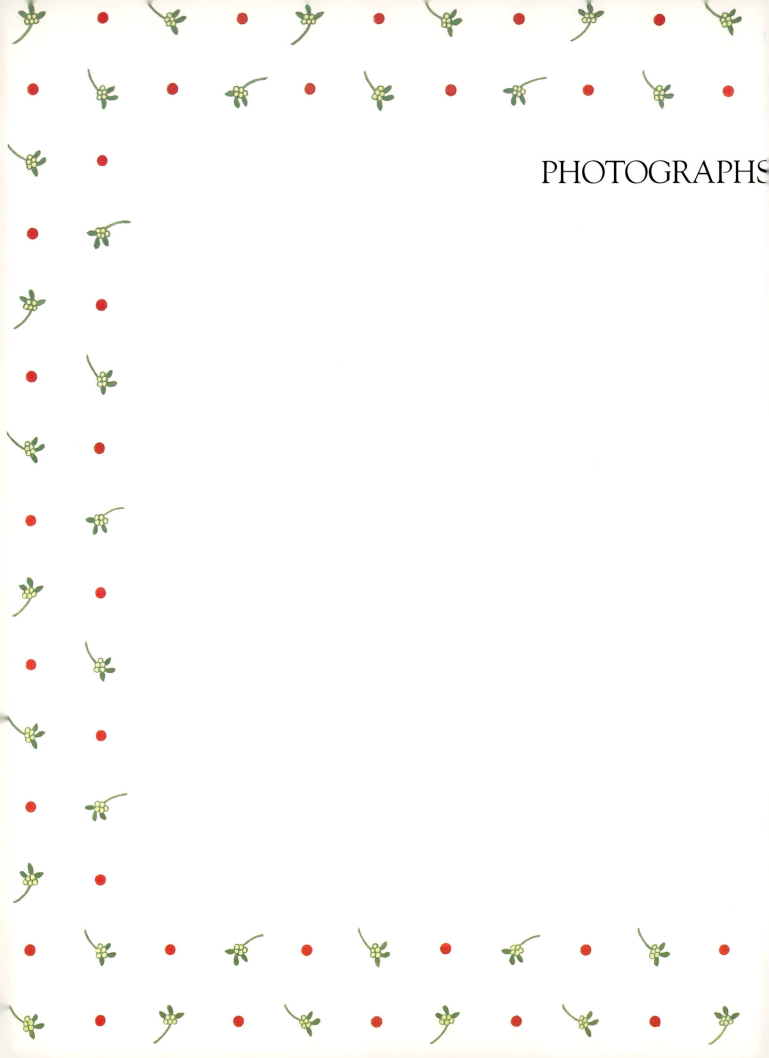

PHOTOGRAPHS

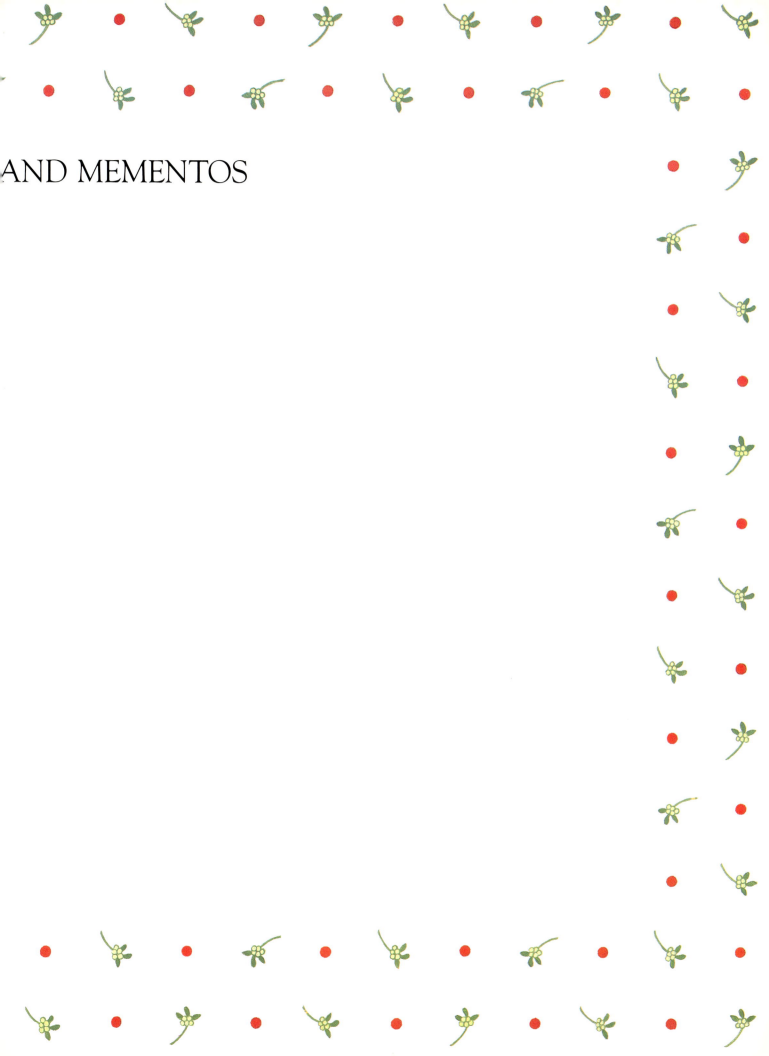

AND MEMENTOS

OUR HOLIDAY SEASON

YEAR

Love and joy come to you,
And to you your wassail too,
And God bless you, and send you
A happy new year.

from an English carol

The events that made this year special were _____

_____

_____

We opened the holiday season by _____

_____

_____

This year we got our house ready for the holidays by _____

_____

_____

DECKING THE HALLS

The tree we chose this year was a _____,

and it was _____ feet tall.

We picked the tree because _____

Helping us decorate were _____

_____

_____

This year we added these new ornaments:

_____

_____

_____

_____

_____

_____

And this is what it looked like:

What made the tree especially beautiful was _____

_____

We celebrated our tree trimming by _____

_____

_____

Other special holiday decorations and arrangements were: _____

_____

_____

HOLIDAY FESTIVITIES

Parties and dinners: _____

_____

_____

_____

_____

_____

Visits and visitors: _____

_____

_____

_____

_____

_____

The best moment came when _____

_____

_____

The prettiest decorations we saw were _____

_____

_____

The best food was _____ served

by _____

Our favorite Christmas card was sent by _____

The best "glad tidings" we received were _____

_____

_____

We really felt the spirit of Christmas when _____

_____

_____

The night before Christmas we _____

_____

_____

_____

_____

_____

_____

_____

_____

_____

CHRISTMAS DAY

Christmas Day fell on a _____ this year, and

the weather was _____

_____ was up first and woke everyone

at _____ o'clock.

Joining us for Christmas were _____

_____

_____

_____

_____

Friends and family who were with us in spirit: _____

_____

_____

_____

The first member of the family to open a present was _____,

who received a _____

from _____

Gifts that made this Christmas special were:

_____	_____	_____
gift	*recipient*	*giver*
_____	_____	_____
gift	*recipient*	*giver*
_____	_____	_____
gift	*recipient*	*giver*
_____	_____	_____
gift	*recipient*	*giver*

The greatest surprise came when _____

_____

This year we spent Christmas day by _____

_____

_____

_____

Our wish for others on this Christmas day: _____

_____

_____

What we will always remember about today is _____

_____

_____

OUR CHRISTMAS DINNER

The meal was prepared by _____

_____

Joining us for dinner were _____

_____

_____

The table was set with _____

_____

The holiday decorations at the table were _____

_____

Everyone agreed that the best dish was _____

_____

What made the dinner special was _____

_____

The perfect ending to a wonderful day was _____

_____

THE
MENU

APPETIZERS: _____

_____

_____

MAIN COURSE: _____

_____

_____

_____

_____

_____

BEVERAGES: _____

_____

_____

DESSERT: _____

_____

_____

OUR HOLIDAY SEASON

YEAR

Happy Christmas to all,
and to all a good night!

Clement C. Moore

The events that made this year special were _____

_____

_____

We opened the holiday season by _____

_____

_____

This year we got our house ready for the holidays by _____

_____

_____

_____

DECKING THE HALLS

The tree we chose this year was a _____,

and it was _____ feet tall.

We picked the tree because _____

Helping us decorate were _____

_____

_____

This year we added these new ornaments:

_____

_____

_____

_____

_____

_____

And this is what it looked like:

What made the tree especially beautiful was _____

_____

We celebrated our tree trimming by _____

_____

_____

Other special holiday decorations and arrangements were: _____

_____

_____

HOLIDAY FESTIVITIES

Parties and dinners: _____
_____
_____
_____
_____

Visits and visitors: _____
_____
_____
_____
_____
_____

The best moment came when _____
_____
_____

The prettiest decorations we saw were _____
_____
_____

The best food was _____ served
by _____

Our favorite Christmas card was sent by _____

The best "glad tidings" we received were _____
_____
_____

We really felt the spirit of Christmas when _____
_____
_____

The night before Christmas we _____
_____
_____

CHRISTMAS DAY

Christmas Day fell on a _____ this year, and

the weather was _____

_____

_____ was up first and woke everyone

at _____ o'clock.

Joining us for Christmas were _____

_____

_____

_____

Friends and family who were with us in spirit: _____

_____

The first member of the family to open a present was _____,

who received a _____

from _____

58

Gifts that made this Christmas special were:

_____   _____   _____
              gift   *recipient*   *giver*

_____   _____   _____
              gift   *recipient*   *giver*

_____   _____   _____
              gift   *recipient*   *giver*

_____   _____   _____
              gift   *recipient*   *giver*

The greatest surprise came when _____

_____

This year we spent Christmas day by _____

_____

_____

Our wish for others on this Christmas day: _____

_____

What we will always remember about today is _____

_____

OUR CHRISTMAS DINNER

The meal was prepared by _____

_____

Joining us for dinner were _____

_____

_____

The table was set with _____

_____

The holiday decorations at the table were _____

_____

Everyone agreed that the best dish was _____

_____

What made the dinner special was _____

_____

The perfect ending to a wonderful day was _____

_____

THE MENU

 A<small>PPETIZERS</small>: _____

_____

_____

M<small>AIN</small> C<small>OURSE</small>: _____

_____

_____

_____

_____

_____

B<small>EVERAGES</small>: _____

_____

_____

D<small>ESSERT</small>: _____

_____

_____

PHOTOGRAPHS

AND MEMENTOS

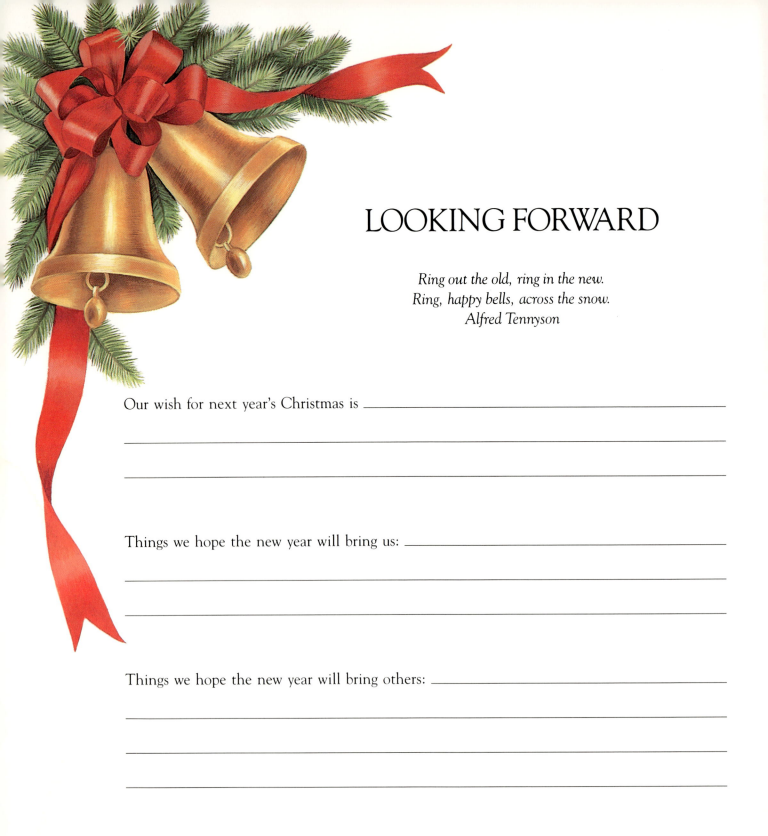

LOOKING FORWARD

Ring out the old, ring in the new.
Ring, happy bells, across the snow.
Alfred Tennyson

Our wish for next year's Christmas is _____

_____

_____

Things we hope the new year will bring us: _____

_____

_____

Things we hope the new year will bring others: _____

_____

_____

_____

(And Happy New Year!)

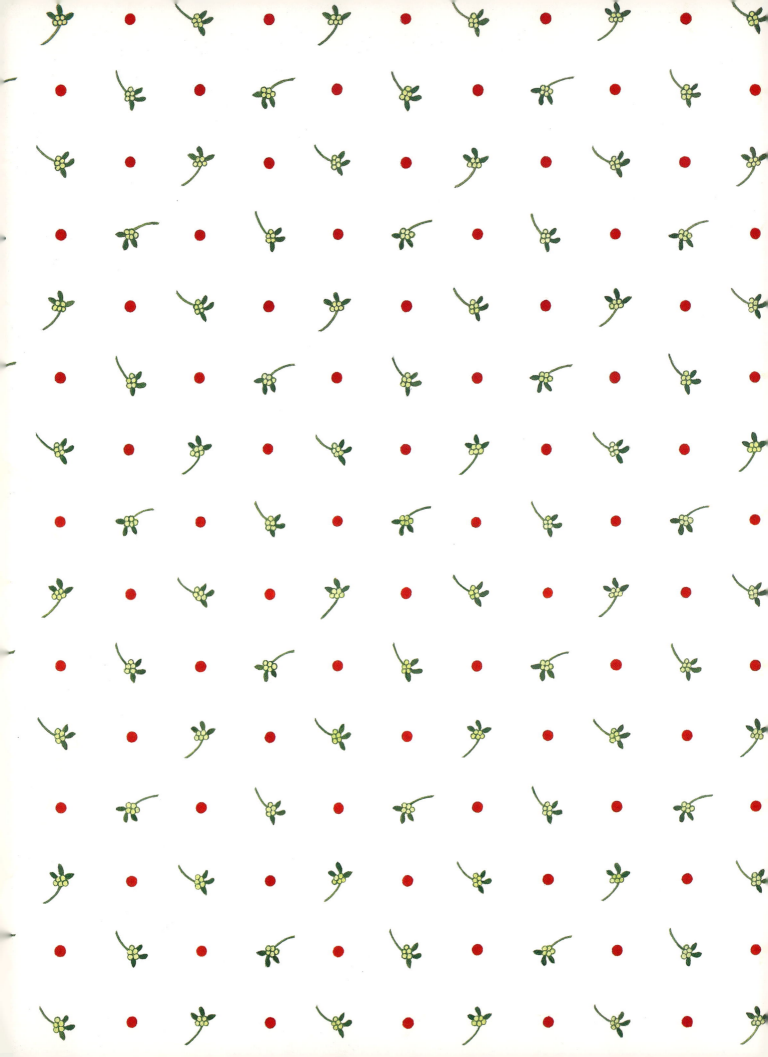